Are you looking for a wonderful baby gift? You can find the perfect blanket to make for your sweet girl or boy in this collection of 8 designs.

Aran **2**

Diamonds **6**

Stripes **10**

Kaleidoscope **12**

Thermal **16**

Hugs & Kisses **18**

Rosebuds **23**

Square-in-Square **26**

General Instructions **29**

Yarn Information **32**

LEISURE ARTS, INC. • Maumelle, Arkansas

aran

EASY Finished Size: 28¼" x 38" (72 cm x 96.5 cm)

SHOPPING LIST
Yarn (Light Weight)
[12.3 ounces, 1,256 yards
(350 grams, 1,148 meters) per skein]:
☐ 2 skeins
Crochet Hook
☐ Size H (5 mm)
 or size needed for gauge
Additional Supplies
☐ Yarn needle

GAUGE INFORMATION
15 hdc and 12 rows = 4" (10 cm)
Popcorn Panel = 8¾"
  (22.25 cm) wide
Twist Cable Panel = 4¼"
  (10.75 cm) wide
Small Cable Panel = 2½"
  (6.25 cm) wide
Gauge Swatch: 4" (10 cm) square
Ch 16.
Row 1: Hdc in second ch from hook and in each ch across: 15 hdc.
Rows 2-12: Ch 1, turn; hdc in each hdc across.
Finish off.

STITCH GUIDE

FRONT POST DOUBLE TREBLE CROCHET *(abbreviated FPdtr)*
YO 3 times, insert hook from **front** to **back** around st indicated *(Fig. 4, page 30)*, YO and pull up a loop (5 loops on hook), (YO and draw through 2 loops on hook) 4 times.

POPCORN (uses one hdc)
5 Hdc in hdc indicated, drop loop from hook, insert hook from **front** to **back** in first hdc of 5-hdc group, hook dropped loop and draw through st.

POPCORN PANEL
Ch 34.

Row 1 (Right side): Hdc in second ch from hook and in each ch across: 33 hdc.

Note: Loop a short piece of yarn around any stitch to mark Row 1 as **right** side **and** bottom edge.

Row 2: Ch 1, turn; hdc in each hdc across.

Row 3: Ch 1, turn; hdc in first hdc, work FPdtr around hdc one row **below** next hdc, skip next hdc from last hdc made, hdc in next 5 hdc, ★ work Popcorn in next hdc, hdc in next 5 hdc; repeat from ★ across to last 2 hdc, work FPdtr around hdc one row **below** next hdc, skip next hdc from last hdc made, hdc in last hdc: 27 hdc, 2 FPdtr, and 4 Popcorns.

2 www.leisurearts.com

Row 4: Ch 1, turn; hdc in each st across: 33 hdc.

Row 5: Ch 1, turn; hdc in first hdc, work FPdtr around FPdtr one row **below** next hdc, skip next hdc from last hdc made, hdc in next 2 hdc, work Popcorn in next hdc, ★ hdc in next 5 hdc, work Popcorn in next hdc; repeat from ★ across to last 4 hdc, hdc in next 2 hdc, work FPdtr around FPdtr one row **below** next hdc, skip next hdc from last hdc made, hdc in last hdc: 26 hdc, 2 FPdtr, and 5 Popcorns.

Row 6: Ch 1, turn; hdc in each st across: 33 hdc.

Row 7: Ch 1, turn; hdc in first hdc, work FPdtr around FPdtr one row **below** next hdc, skip next hdc from last hdc made, hdc in next 5 hdc, ★ work Popcorn in next hdc, hdc in next 5 hdc; repeat from ★ across to last 2 hdc, work FPdtr around FPdtr one row **below** next hdc, skip next hdc from last hdc made, hdc in last hdc: 27 hdc, 2 FPdtr, and 4 Popcorns.

Repeat Rows 4-7 for pattern until Panel measures approximately 37" (94 cm) from beginning ch, ending by working Row 6; finish off.

TWIST CABLE PANEL
(Make 2)
Ch 17.

Row 1 (Right side)**:** Hdc in second ch from hook and in each ch across: 16 hdc.

Note: Mark Row 1 as **right** side **and** bottom edge.

Row 2: Ch 1, turn; hdc in each hdc across.

Row 3: Ch 1, turn; hdc in first hdc, work FPdtr around hdc one row **below** next hdc, skip next hdc from last hdc made, hdc in next 4 hdc, skip next 6 hdc two rows **below** from last FPdtr made, work FPdtr around each of next 2 hdc, working in **front** of last FPdtr made, work FPdtr around fifth and sixth skipped hdc two rows **below**, skip next 4 hdc from last hdc made, hdc in next 4 hdc, work FPdtr around hdc one row **below** next hdc, skip next hdc from last hdc made, hdc in last hdc: 10 hdc and 6 FPdtr.

Row 4: Ch 1, turn; hdc in each st across: 16 hdc.

4 www.leisurearts.com

Row 5: Ch 1, turn; hdc in first hdc, work FPdtr around FPdtr one row **below** next hdc, skip next hdc from last hdc made, hdc in next 4 hdc, work FPdtr around each of next 4 FPdtr two rows **below**, skip next 4 hdc from last hdc made, hdc in next 4 hdc, work FPdtr around FPdtr one row **below** next hdc, skip next hdc from last hdc made, hdc in last hdc: 10 hdc and 6 FPdtr.

Row 6: Ch 1, turn; hdc in each st across: 16 hdc.

Row 7: Ch 1, turn; hdc in first hdc, work FPdtr around FPdtr one row **below** next hdc, skip next hdc from last hdc made, hdc in next 4 hdc, skip next 2 FPdtr two rows **below**, work FPdtr around each of next 2 FPdtr, working in **front** of last FPdtr made, work FPdtr around each of 2 skipped FPdtr, skip next 4 hdc from last hdc made, hdc in next 4 hdc, work FPdtr around FPdtr one row **below** next hdc, skip next hdc from last hdc made, hdc in last hdc: 10 hdc and 6 FPdtr.

Repeat Rows 4-7 for pattern until Panel measures approximately 37" (94 cm) from beginning ch, ending by working Row 6; finish off.

SMALL CABLE PANEL
(Make 4)

Ch 10.

Row 1 (Right side)**:** Hdc in second ch from hook and in each ch across: 9 hdc.

Note: Mark Row 1 as **right** side **and** bottom edge.

Row 2: Ch 1, turn; hdc in each hdc across.

Row 3: Ch 1, turn; hdc in first hdc, work FPdtr around hdc one row **below** next hdc, skip next hdc from last hdc made, hdc in next 3 hdc, [ch 3, slip st around hdc one row **below** next hdc just made, hdc in each ch just made **(Cable made)**], hdc in next 2 hdc, work FPdtr around hdc one row **below** next hdc, skip next hdc from last hdc made, hdc in last hdc: one Cable, 7 hdc, and 2 FPdtr.

Row 4: Ch 1, turn; hdc in each st across: 9 hdc.

Row 5: Ch 1, turn; hdc in first hdc, work FPdtr around FPdtr one row **below** next hdc, skip next hdc from last hdc made, hdc in next 3 hdc, [ch 3, slip st around hdc **before** Cable in previous Cable row, hdc in each ch just made **(Cable made)**], hdc in next 2 hdc, work FPdtr around FPdtr one row **below** next hdc, skip next hdc from last hdc made, hdc in last hdc: one Cable, 7 hdc, and 2 FPdtr.

Repeat Rows 4 and 5 for pattern until Panel measures approximately 37" (94 cm) from beginning ch, ending by working Row 4; finish off.

ASSEMBLY

Place the panels in the following order: Small Cable, Twist Cable, Small Cable, Popcorn, Small Cable, Twist Cable, and Small Cable.

Hold two panels with **right** sides facing and bottom edges at same end. Weave panels together *(Fig. 8, page 31)*.

Join remaining panels in same manner.

EDGING

Rnd 1: With **right** side facing, join yarn with hdc in first hdc on top edge *(see Joining With Hdc, page 30)*; 2 hdc in same st, hdc in next hdc and in each hdc across to last hdc, 3 hdc in last hdc; work 123 hdc evenly spaced across ends of rows; working in free loops of beginning chs *(Fig. 3, page 30)*, 3 hdc in first ch, hdc in each ch across to last ch, 3 hdc in last ch; work 123 hdc evenly spaced across ends of rows; join with slip st to first hdc: 456 hdc.

Rnd 2: Ch 2, do **not** turn; working from **left** to **right**, work reverse hdc in same st *(Figs. 9a-d, page 31)*, ch 1, skip next hdc, ★ † work reverse hdc in next hdc, ch 1, skip next hdc †; repeat from † to † across to next corner 3-hdc group, (work reverse hdc in next hdc, ch 1) 3 times, skip next hdc; repeat from ★ 2 times **more**, then repeat from † to † across to last 2 hdc, (work reverse hdc in next hdc, ch 1) twice; join with slip st to first st, finish off.

Design by Carole Rutter Tippett.

diamonds

EASY Finished Size: 38½" x 52½" (98 cm x 133.5 cm)

SHOPPING LIST
Yarn (Light Weight) [3]
[4.5 ounces, 318 yards
(127 grams, 290 meters) per skein]:
☐ Grey - 4 skeins
☐ Green - 2 skeins
☐ Peach - 2 skeins

Crochet Hook
☐ Size G (4 mm)
  or size needed for gauge

Additional Supplies
☐ Yarn needle

GAUGE INFORMATION
Each Block = 6¾" (17.25 cm)
Gauge Swatch: 3¼" (from straight edges to straight edges) x 4¾" (from point to point) (8.25 cm x 12 cm)
Work same as Diamond: 38 dc and 6 sps.

STITCH GUIDE
TREBLE CROCHET *(abbreviated tr)*
YO twice, insert hook in st indicated, YO and pull up a loop (4 loops on hook), (YO and draw through 2 loops on hook) 3 times.

BLOCK A (Make 18)
DIAMOND (Make 4)
Rnd 1 (Right side)**:** With Green ch 4, 4 dc in fourth ch from hook **(3 skipped chs count as first dc, now and throughout)**, ch 3, 5 dc in same ch, ch 3; join with slip st to first dc: 10 dc and 2 ch-3 sps.

Note: Loop a short piece of yarn around any stitch to mark Rnd 1 as **right** side.

Rnd 2: Ch 3 **(counts as first dc, now and throughout)**, † (3 dc in next dc, dc in next dc) twice, (2 dc, ch 3, 2 dc) in next ch-3 sp †, dc in next dc, repeat from † to † once; join with slip st to first dc, finish off: 26 dc and 2 ch-3 sps.

Rnd 3: With **right** side facing, join Grey with dc in either ch-3 sp *(see Joining With Dc, page 30)*; (dc, ch 3, 2 dc) in same sp, † dc in next 4 dc, (dc, ch 1, dc) in next dc, dc in next 3 dc, (dc, ch 1, dc) in next dc, dc in next 4 dc †, (2 dc, ch 3, 2 dc) in next ch-3 sp, repeat from † to † once; join with slip st to first dc, finish off: 38 dc and 6 sps.

BLOCK ASSEMBLY

With Grey and using Block Diagram as a guide for placement, whipstitch 4 Diamonds together *(Fig. 7a, page 31)*, working in **both** loops on **both** pieces and beginning in center ch of first ch-3 and ending in next ch-1.

BLOCK DIAGRAM

BLOCK B (Make 17)

Work same as Block A substituting Peach for Green.

SMALL SQUARE (Make 58)

Rnd 1 (Right side)**:** With Grey, ch 4, 2 dc in fourth ch from hook, ch 3, (3 dc in same ch, ch 3) 3 times; join with slip st to first dc, finish off leaving a long end for sewing: 12 dc and 4 ch-3 sps.

Note: Mark Rnd 1 as **right** side.

TRIANGLE (Make 24)

Row 1 (Right side)**:** With Grey, ch 6, (3 dc, ch 3, 3 dc, ch 1, tr) in sixth ch from hook (**5 skipped chs count as first tr plus ch 1**); finish off leaving a long end for sewing: 8 sts and 3 sps.

Note: Mark Row 1 as **right** side.

ASSEMBLY

Using Placement Diagram as a guide, with Grey, whipstitch Blocks together forming 5 vertical strips of 7 Blocks each, working in **both** loops on **both** pieces and beginning in center ch of first ch-3 and ending in next ch-1 on first Diamond, then beginning in first ch-1 and ending in center ch of next ch-3 on next Diamond.

Whipstitch strips together in same manner.

Whipstitch Small Squares in place between Blocks, matching corner chs and using long end.

Whipstitch Triangles to outer edges, using long end and beginning in last tr on Triangle and corresponding ch on Block and ending in first tr on Triangle and corresponding ch on same Block.

EDGING

Rnd 1: With **right** side facing, join Grey with dc in any corner ch-3 sp; ch 3, 2 dc in same sp, ★ dc in next 7 dc and in same ch as joining, ch 1; working across next Triangle, hdc in end of first tr, ch 1, hdc in center ch, ch 1, hdc in end of last tr, ch 1; working across next Diamond, dc in same ch as joining and in next 7 dc, † dc in next sp, dc in joining and in next sp, dc in next 7 dc and in same ch as joining, ch 1; working across next Triangle, hdc in end of first tr, ch 1, hdc in center ch, ch 1, hdc in end of last tr, ch 1; working across next Diamond, dc in same ch as joining and in next 7 dc †; repeat from † to † across to next corner ch-3 sp, (2 dc, ch 3, 2 dc) in corner ch-3 sp; repeat from ★ 2 times **more**, dc in next 7 dc and in same ch as joining, ch 1; working across next Triangle, hdc in end of first tr, ch 1, hdc in center ch, ch 1, hdc in end of last tr, ch 1; working across next Diamond, dc in same ch as joining and in next 7 dc, repeat from † to † across, dc in same sp as first dc; join with slip st to first dc: 532 sts and 100 sps.

Rnd 2: (Slip st, ch 3, dc, ch 3, 2 dc) in first corner ch-3 sp, working in sts and in chs, ★ dc in next dc and in each st across to next corner ch-3 sp, (2 dc, ch 3, 2 dc) in corner ch-3 sp; repeat from ★ 2 times **more**, dc in next dc and in each st across; join with slip st to first dc: 644 dc and 4 corner ch-3 sps.

Rnd 3: Slip st in next dc, ch 4 (**counts as first dc plus ch 1**), (dc, ch 3, dc) in next corner ch-3 sp, ch 1, ★ dc in next dc, ch 1, (skip next dc, dc in next dc, ch 1) across to next corner ch-3 sp, (dc, ch 3, dc) in corner ch-3 sp, ch 1; repeat from ★ 2 times **more**, (dc in next dc, ch 1, skip next st) across; join with slip st to first dc.

Rnd 4: Ch 1, hdc in same st as joining, (slip st, ch 1, hdc) in next dc, skip next ch, (slip st, ch 1, hdc) in next ch (center ch), ★ (slip st, ch 1, hdc) in next dc and in each dc across to next corner ch-3, skip next ch, (slip st, ch 1, hdc) in next ch (center ch); repeat from ★ 2 times **more**, (slip st, ch 1, hdc) in next dc and in each dc across; join with slip st to joining slip st, finish off.

Design by Anne Halliday.

PLACEMENT DIAGRAM

stripes

EASY Finished Size: 34" x 45½" (86.5 cm x 115.5 cm)

SHOPPING LIST
Yarn (Light Weight) [3]
[5 ounces, 459 yards
(140 grams, 420 meters) per skein]:
☐ Peach - 2 skeins
☐ White - 2 skeins
Crochet Hook
☐ Size G (4 mm)
 or size needed for gauge

GAUGE INFORMATION
In pattern, 17 dc = 4" (10 cm);
 2 repeats (Rows 1-10) = 3¾"
 (9.5 cm)
Gauge Swatch: 4¼" wide x 3¾" high
 (10.75 cm x 9.5 cm)
With Peach, ch 18.
Work same as Body for 10 rows:
18 dc.
Finish off.

STITCH GUIDE
PICOT
Ch 3, slip st in third ch from hook.

BODY
Each row is worked across length of Body.

With White, ch 190.

Row 1: Sc in second ch from hook, ★ ch 5, skip next 3 chs, sc in next ch; repeat from ★ across: 48 sc and 47 ch-5 sps.

Row 2 (Right side): Ch 5 (**counts as first dc plus ch 2, now and throughout**), turn; sc in next ch-5 sp, (ch 5, sc in next ch-5 sp) across, ch 2, dc in last sc: 48 sps.

*Note: Loop a short piece of yarn around any stitch to mark Row 2 as **right** side.*

Row 3: Ch 1, turn; sc in first dc, ch 3, skip next ch-2 sp, sc in next ch-5 sp, (ch 3, sc in next ch-5 sp) across to last ch-2 sp, ch 3, skip last ch-2 sp, sc in last dc changing to Peach *(Fig. 5a, page 30)*; do **not** cut White: 47 ch-3 sps.

Carry unused yarn loosely along the edge.

Row 4: Ch 3, turn; 4 dc in each ch-3 sp across to last sc, dc in last sc: 190 dc.

Row 5: Ch 3, turn; dc in next dc and in each dc across changing to White in last dc *(Fig. 5b, page 30)*; cut Peach.

Row 6: Ch 1, turn; sc in first dc, ★ ch 5, skip next 4 dc, sc in sp **before** next dc *(Fig. 6, page 31)*; repeat from ★ across to last 5 dc, ch 5, skip next 4 dc, sc in last dc: 47 ch-5 sps.

Row 7: Ch 5, turn; sc in next ch-5 sp, (ch 5, sc in next ch-5 sp) across, ch 2, dc in last sc: 48 sps.

Row 8: Ch 1, turn; sc in first dc, ch 3, skip next ch-2 sp, sc in next ch-5 sp, (ch 3, sc in next ch-5 sp) across to last ch-2 sp, ch 3, skip last ch-2 sp, sc in last dc changing to Peach; do **not** cut White: 47 ch-3 sps.

Rows 9-88: Repeat Rows 4-8, 16 times; at end of Row 88, do **not** change colors and do **not** finish off White: 47 ch-3 sps.

EDGING
Work around carried yarn along edges.

Rnd 1: Do **not** turn; (sc, work Picot, sc) in last sc on Row 88, † working in ends of rows, sc in next 2 rows, work Picot, sc in next dc row, 2 sc in next dc row, work Picot, ♥ sc in next 3 rows, work Picot, sc in next dc row, 2 sc in next dc row, work Picot ♥; repeat from ♥ to ♥ across to last 3 rows, sc in next 2 rows, skip last row †; (sc, work Picot, sc) in free loop of ch at base of first sc *(Fig. 3, page 30)*, working in sps across beginning ch, 2 sc in next sp, work Picot, (3 sc in next sp, work Picot) across to last sp, 2 sc in last sp, (sc, work Picot, sc) in last ch, repeat from † to † once, (sc, work Picot, sc) in first sc on Row 88, 2 sc in next ch-3 sp, work Picot, (3 sc in next ch-3 sp, work Picot) across to last ch-3 sp, 2 sc in last sp; join with slip st to first sc, finish off.

Design by Melissa Leapman.

kaleidoscope

EASY Finished Size: 46½" (118 cm) square

SHOPPING LIST

Yarn (Medium Weight)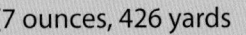
[7 ounces, 426 yards
(197 grams, 389 meters) per skein]:
- ☐ Yellow - 3 skeins
- ☐ Blue - 2 skeins
- ☐ Light Blue - 1 skein
- ☐ Dark Blue - 1 skein

Crochet Hook
- ☐ Size H (5 mm)
   or size needed for gauge

Additional Supplies
- ☐ Yarn needle

GAUGE INFORMATION

Gauge Swatch: 4½" (11.5 cm) square
Work same as Square on page 14.

STITCH GUIDE

FRONT POST DOUBLE CROCHET *(abbreviated FPdc)*
YO, insert hook from **front** to **back** around post of st indicated *(Fig. 4, page 30)*, YO and pull up a loop (3 loops on hook), (YO and draw through 2 loops on hook) twice.

BACK POST DOUBLE CROCHET *(abbreviated BPdc)*
YO, insert hook from **back** to **front** around post of st indicated *(Fig. 4, page 30)*, YO and pull up a loop (3 loops on hook), (YO and draw through 2 loops on hook) twice.

DOUBLE CROCHET 2 TOGETHER *(abbreviated dc2tog)* (uses next 2 dc)
★ YO, insert hook in **next** dc, YO and pull up a loop, YO and draw through 2 loops on hook; repeat from ★ once **more**, YO and draw through all 3 loops on hook (**counts as one dc**).

DOUBLE CROCHET 3 TOGETHER *(abbreviated dc3tog)* (uses next 3 dc)
★ YO, insert hook in **next** dc, YO and pull up a loop, YO and draw through 2 loops on hook; repeat from ★ 2 times **more**, YO and draw through all 4 loops on hook (**counts as one dc**).

SQUARE (Make 100 total)

Make 32 **each** of Square A **and** Square C, and 36 of Square B.

Rows	A	B	C
1-4	Blue	Dk Blue	Lt Blue
5-8	Yellow	Yellow	Yellow
9-12	Lt Blue	Blue	Dk Blue

Row 1: With first color indicated, ch 4, 3 dc in fourth ch from hook **(3 skipped chs count as first dc)**: 4 dc.

Row 2 (Right side): Ch 3 **(counts as first dc, now and throughout)**, turn; dc in first dc, work FPdc around each of next 2 dc, 2 dc in last dc: 6 sts.

Note: Loop a short piece of yarn around any stitch to mark Row 2 as **right** side.

Row 3: Ch 3, turn; 2 dc in first dc, dc in next dc, work BPdc around next FPdc, ch 1, work BPdc around next FPdc, dc in next dc, 3 dc in last dc: 10 sts and one ch-1 sp.

Row 4: Ch 3, turn; 2 dc in first dc, dc in next 3 dc, work FPdc around next BPdc, ch 1, work FPdc around next BPdc, dc in next 3 dc, 3 dc in last dc changing to next color in last dc *(Fig. 5b, page 30)*: 14 sts and one ch-1 sp.

Row 5: Ch 3, turn; 2 dc in first dc, dc in next 5 dc, work BPdc around next FPdc, ch 1, work BPdc around next FPdc, dc in next 5 dc, 3 dc in last dc: 18 sts and one ch-1 sp.

Row 6: Ch 3, turn; 2 dc in first dc, dc in next 7 dc, work FPdc around next BPdc, ch 1, work FPdc around next BPdc, dc in next 7 dc, 3 dc in last dc: 22 sts and one ch-1 sp.

Row 7: Ch 2, turn; dc2tog, dc in next 7 dc, work BPdc around next FPdc, ch 1, work BPdc around next FPdc, dc in next 7 dc, dc3tog: 18 sts and one ch-1 sp.

Row 8: Ch 2, turn; dc2tog, dc in next 5 dc, work FPdc around next BPdc, ch 1, work FPdc around next BPdc, dc in next 5 dc, dc3tog changing to next color: 14 sts and one ch-1 sp.

Row 9: Ch 2, turn; dc2tog, dc in next 3 dc, work BPdc around next FPdc, ch 1, work BPdc around next FPdc, dc in next 3 dc, dc3tog: 10 sts and one ch-1 sp.

Row 10: Ch 2, turn; dc2tog, dc in next dc, work FPdc around next BPdc, ch 1, work FPdc around next BPdc, dc in next dc, dc3tog: 6 sts and one ch-1 sp.

Row 11: Ch 2, turn; dc in next dc, work BPdc around each of next 2 FPdc, dc2tog: 4 sts.

Row 12: Ch 2, turn; ★ YO, insert hook from **front** to **back** around post of **next** BPdc, YO and pull up a loop, YO and draw through 2 loops on hook; repeat from ★ once **more**, YO, insert hook in last dc, YO and pull up a loop (5 loops on hook), YO and draw through 2 loops on hook, YO and draw through all 4 loops on hook; finish off.

ASSEMBLY

Using Placement Diagram as a guide, with **wrong** sides together, whipstitch Squares *(Fig. A)* together forming 10 vertical strips of 10 Squares each, beginning in first corner and ending in next corner; then join strips together in same manner.

Fig. A

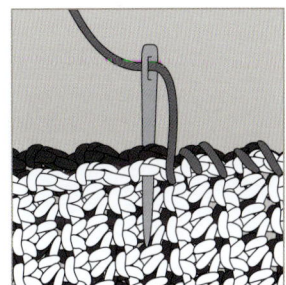

EDGING

Rnd 1: With **right** side facing, join Blue with sc in any corner *(see Joining With Sc, page 30)*; 2 sc in same st, ★ † work 12 sc evenly spaced across same Square, work 13 sc evenly spaced across each of next 9 Squares †, 3 sc in corner; repeat from ★ 2 times **more**, then repeat from † to † once; join with slip st to first sc: 528 sc.

Rnd 2: Ch 3, (sc, dc, sc) in next sc, ★ dc in next sc, (sc in next sc, dc in next sc) across to next corner sc, (sc, dc, sc) in corner sc; repeat from ★ 2 times **more**, (dc in next sc, sc in next sc) across; join with slip st to first dc: 536 sts.

Rnd 3: Ch 1, sc in same st as joining, dc in next sc, (sc, dc, sc) in next dc, ★ dc in next sc, (sc in next dc, dc in next sc) across to next corner dc, (sc, dc, sc) in corner dc; repeat from ★ 2 times **more**, dc in next sc, (sc in next sc, dc in next sc) across; join with slip st to first sc, finish off.

Design by Jennine DeMoss.

PLACEMENT DIAGRAM

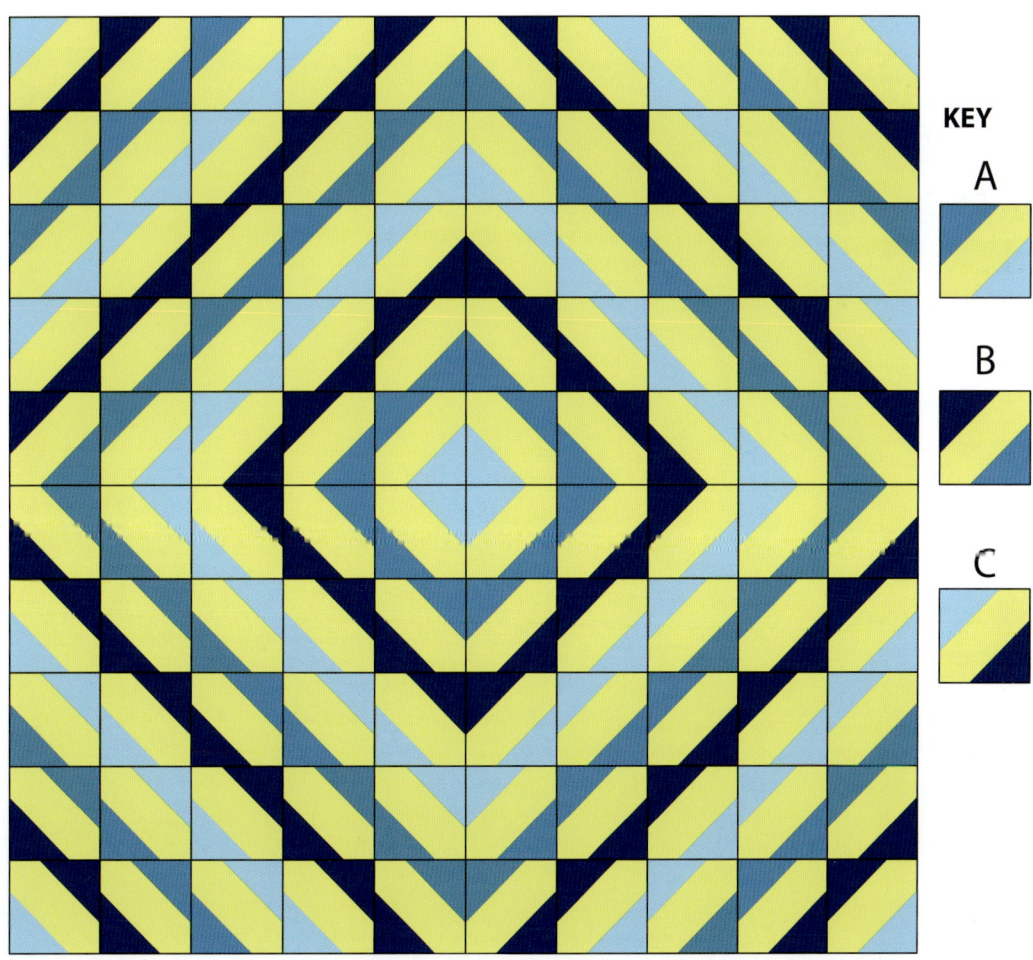

KEY

A

B

C

15

thermal

EASY +   **Finished Size:** 25½" x 32" (65 cm x 81.5 cm)

SHOPPING LIST

Yarn (Light Weight) [3]
[5 ounces, 362 yards
(140 grams, 331 meters) per skein]:
☐ White - 2 skeins
☐ Pink - 2 skeins

Crochet Hooks
Double-ended hook,
☐ Size H (5 mm)
or size needed for gauge
Standard hook (for Edging only),
☐ Size H (5 mm)

GAUGE INFORMATION

In pattern, 17 sts = 4" (10 cm);
17 rows = 2" (5 cm)
Gauge Swatch: 4" wide x 2⅛" high
(10 cm x 5.5 cm)
With double-ended hook and Pink,
ch 18.

Note: Because you are working with fewer loops, you will need to slide the loops to the opposite end of the hook before turning.

Work same as Body for 18 rows. Finish off and cut White.

16   www.leisurearts.com

BODY

With double-ended hook and Pink, ch 100, drop Pink.

Row 1: With White and working in top loop of each ch *(Fig. A)*, insert hook in second ch from hook, YO and pull up a loop, (insert hook in next ch, YO and pull up a loop) across; drop White: 100 loops.

Fig. A

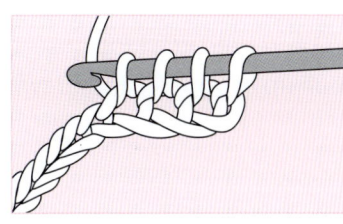

Row 2: Turn; with Pink, YO and draw through one loop on hook, ★ YO and draw through 2 loops on hook *(Fig. B)*; repeat from ★ across until one loop remains on hook; drop Pink: 100 vertical bars.

Fig. B

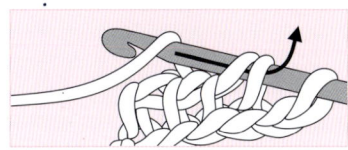

Row 3: With White, ch 1, do **not** turn; skip first vertical bar, ★ insert hook under next vertical bar *(Fig. C)*, YO and pull up a loop; repeat from ★ across; drop White: 100 loops.

Fig. C

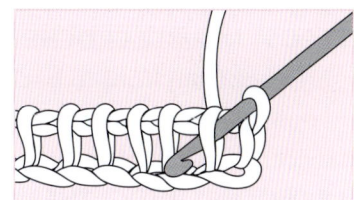

Repeat Rows 2 and 3 for pattern until Body measures approximately 30" (76 cm) from beginning ch, ending by working Row 2; at end of last row, cut White and do **not** drop Pink.

Last Row (Right side)**:** Ch 1, do **not** turn; sc under each vertical bar across; finish off: 100 sc.

Note: Loop a short piece of yarn around any stitch to mark Last Row as **right** side.

EDGING

Rnd 1: With **right** side facing and using standard hook, join White with sc in first sc on Last Row *(see Joining With Sc, page 30)*; sc in same st, 2 sc in next sc, sc in each sc across to last sc, 3 sc in last sc; work 129 sc evenly spaced across ends of rows; working in free loops of beginning ch *(Fig. 3, page 30)*, 3 sc in first ch, 2 sc in next ch, sc in each ch across to last ch, 3 sc in last ch; work 129 sc evenly spaced across ends of rows; sc in same st as first sc; join with slip st to first sc: 468 sc.

Rnd 2: Do **not** turn; skip next 2 sc, 7 dc in next sc, skip next 2 sc, ★ slip st in next sc, skip next 2 sc, 7 dc in next sc, skip next 2 sc; repeat from ★ around; join with slip st to joining slip st, finish off.

Design by Leigh K. Nestor.

EASY + Finished Size: 35¾" x 46" (91 cm x 117 cm)

SHOPPING LIST
Yarn (Fine Weight) 🧶2
[3.5 ounces, 317 yards
(100 grams, 290 meters) per skein]:
- ☐ White - 5 skeins
- ☐ Blue - 4 skeins
- ☐ Yellow - 1 skein

Crochet Hook
- ☐ Size G (4 mm)
  or size needed for gauge

Additional Supplies
- ☐ Tapestry needle

GAUGE INFORMATION
Each Motif (from point to point) =
 2³⁄₈" (6 cm)
Each Strip = 3¾" (9.5 cm) wide
Gauge Swatch: 2³⁄₈" (6 cm)
Work same as First Motif.

STITCH GUIDE

FRONT POST DOUBLE CROCHET *(abbreviated FPdc)*
YO, insert hook from **front** to **back** around post of st indicated *(Fig. 4, page 30)*, YO and pull up a loop (3 loops on hook), (YO and draw through 2 loops on hook) twice. Skip sc **behind** FPdc.

SINGLE CROCHET 2 TOGETHER *(abbreviated sc2tog)*
Insert hook in same sc as seam on same Strip, YO and pull up a loop, insert hook in same sc as seam on next Strip, YO and pull up a loop, YO and draw through all 3 loops on hook (**counts as one sc**).

PICOT
Ch 3, slip st in third ch from hook.

STRIP (Make 9)
FIRST MOTIF
CENTER BLOCK
With White, ch 5.

Row 1 (Right side):
Step 1 - Insert hook in back ridge of second ch from hook *(Fig. 1, page 30)*, YO and pull up a loop, ★ insert hook in back ridge of next ch, YO and pull up a loop; repeat from ★ across: 5 loops.
Step 2 - YO and draw through one loop on hook, ★ YO and draw through 2 loops on hook *(Fig. B, page 17)*; repeat from ★ across until one loop remains: 5 vertical bars.

Note: Loop a short piece of yarn around any stitch to mark Row 1 as **right** side.

Rows 2 and 3:
Step 1 - Skip first vertical bar, insert hook under next vertical bar *(Fig. C, page 17)*, YO and pull up a loop, (insert hook under next vertical bar, YO and pull up a loop) across: 5 loops.
Step 2 - YO and draw through one loop on hook, (YO and draw through 2 loops on hook) across until one loop remains: 5 vertical bars.

Row 4:
Ch 1, skip first vertical bar, slip st under next vertical bar and under each vertical bar across; do **not** finish off.

FIRST BLOCK
Ch 5.

Row 1:
Step 1 - Insert hook in back ridge of second ch from hook, YO and pull up a loop, ★ insert hook in back ridge of next ch, YO and pull up a loop; repeat from ★ across: 5 loops.
Step 2 - YO and draw through one loop on hook, ★ YO and draw through 2 loops on hook; repeat from ★ across until one loop remains: 5 vertical bars.

Rows 2 and 3:
Step 1 - Skip first vertical bar, insert hook under next vertical bar, YO and pull up a loop, (insert hook under next vertical bar, YO and pull up a loop) across: 5 loops.
Step 2 - YO and draw through one loop on hook, ★ YO and draw through 2 loops on hook; repeat from ★ across until one loop remains: 5 vertical bars.

Row 4:
Ch 1, skip first vertical bar, slip st under next vertical bar and under each vertical bar across, slip st in next corner on Center Block; do **not** finish off.

SECOND & THIRD BLOCKS
Work same as First Block.

FOURTH BLOCK
Work same as First Block; at end of Row 4, slip st in corner sp between Center Block and First Block; finish off.

DIAGRAM

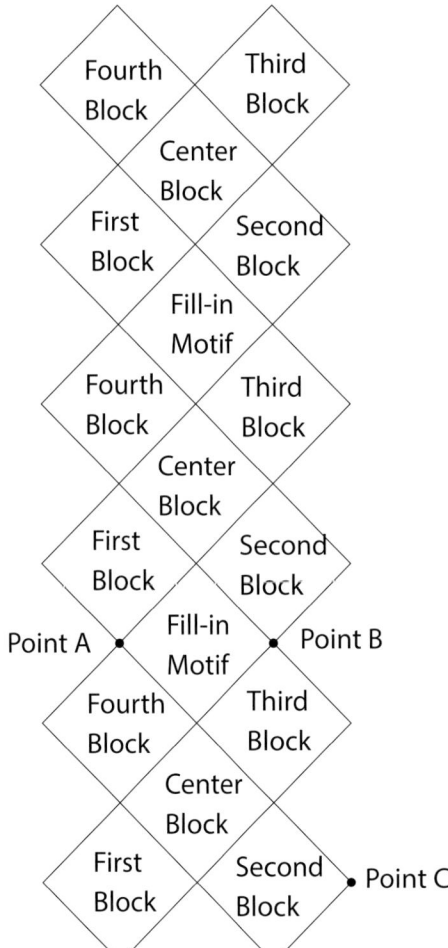

SECOND THRU EIGHTEENTH MOTIFS
CENTER BLOCK
Work same as Center Block of First Motif.

FIRST BLOCK
Work same as First Block of First Motif through Row 3; drop loop from hook, insert hook in top corner of Fourth Block on previous Motif (Point A on Diagram), hook dropped loop and draw through st.

Row 4: Ch 1, skip first vertical bar, slip st under next vertical bar and each vertical bar across, slip st in next corner on Center Block; do **not** finish off.

SECOND BLOCK
Ch 5, drop loop from hook, insert hook in top corner of Third Block on First Motif (Point B on Diagram), hook dropped loop and draw through st.

Rows 1-4: Repeat Rows 1-4 of Second Block of First Motif.

THIRD & FOURTH BLOCKS
Work same as Third and Fourth Blocks of First Motif.

CENTER RING
Rnd 1: With **right** side facing and working in ends of rows on Blocks around Center Block, join Yellow with slip st in any row; slip st in each row around; do **not** join, place marker to mark beginning of rnd *(see Markers, page 30)*.

Rnd 2: Slip st in each slip st around; finish off.

Repeat Center Ring on each Motif.

FILL-IN MOTIF
With Blue, ch 3, slip st in st in valley between two Blocks, ch 2, slip st in first ch made, ★ ch 2, slip st in st in valley between two Blocks, ch 2, slip st in first ch made; repeat from ★ 2 times **more**; finish off.

Repeat Fill-in Motif between Motifs.

BORDER
Rnd 1: With **right** side facing and working across long edge, join Blue with sc in corner of Second Block on First Motif (Point C on Diagram) *(see Joining With Sc, page 30)*; † ch 3, dc in st in valley between Blocks, ch 3, sc in corner of next Block †; repeat from † to † across, ch 4 (corner), sc in next corner of **same** Block, ch 3, dc in st in valley between Blocks, ch 3, sc in corner of next Block, ch 4 (corner), sc in next corner of **same** Block, repeat from † to † across, ch 4 (corner), sc in next corner of **same** Block, ch 3, dc in st in valley between Blocks, ch 3, sc in corner of last Block, ch 4 (corner); join with slip st to first sc: 148 sts, 144 ch-3 sps, and 4 corner ch-4 sps.

Rnd 2: Ch 3 (**counts as first dc**), † ★ 2 dc in next ch-3 sp, dc in next dc, 2 dc in next ch-3 sp, dc in next sc; repeat from ★ across to next corner ch-4 sp, (3 dc, ch 3, 3 dc) in corner ch-4 sp, dc in next sc, 2 dc in next ch-3 sp, dc in next dc, 2 dc in next ch-3 sp, dc in next sc, (3 dc, ch 3, 3 dc) in next corner ch-4 sp †, dc in next sc, repeat from † to † once; join with slip st to first dc, finish off: 460 dc and 4 corner ch-3 sps.

Rnd 3: With **right** side facing, join White with sc in same st as joining; ★ sc in each dc across to next corner ch-3 sp, 3 sc in corner ch-3 sp; repeat from ★ 3 times **more**, sc in last 3 dc; join with slip st to Back Loop Only of first sc *(Fig. 2, page 30)*: 472 sc.

Rnd 4: Ch 1, working in Back Loops Only of sc, sc in same st as joining and in next 2 sc, work FPdc around dc one rnd **below** next sc, (sc in next 5 sc, work FPdc around dc one rnd **below** next sc) across to within 6 sc of next corner 3-sc group, † sc in next 7 sc, 3 sc in next sc, sc in next 7 sc, work FPdc around dc one rnd **below** next sc †; repeat from † to † once **more**, (sc in next 5 sc, work FPdc around dc one rnd **below** next sc) across to within 6 sc of next corner 3-sc group, repeat from † to † once, sc in next 7 sc, 3 sc in next sc, sc in last 4 sc; join with slip st to **both** loops of first sc, finish off: 480 sts.

ASSEMBLY

Join Strips together as follows:

With **wrong** sides together, whipstitch strips together with White *(Fig. 7b, page 31)*, beginning and ending in corner sc and working through **inside** loops only on **both** pieces.

Join remaining Strips in same manner.

EDGING

Rnd 1: With **right** side facing and working across top edge, join Blue with sc in center sc of first corner 3-sc group; 2 sc in same st, † sc in next 17 sts, (sc2tog, sc in next 17 sts) across to next corner sc, 3 sc in corner sc †, sc in each st across to next corner sc, 3 sc in corner sc, repeat from † to † once, sc in each st across; join with slip st to first sc, finish off: 776 sc.

Rnd 2: With **right** side facing and working in Back Loops Only, join White with sc in any corner sc; 2 sc in same st, ★ sc in each sc across to next corner sc, 3 sc in corner sc; repeat from ★ 2 times **more**, sc in each sc across; join with slip st to **both** loops of first sc, finish off: 784 sc.

Rnd 3: With **right** side facing, join Blue with sc in first sc of any corner 3-sc group; work Picot, (sc in next sc, work Picot) twice, ★ skip next sc, (sc in next sc, work Picot, skip next sc) across to next corner 3-sc group, (sc in next sc, work Picot) 3 times; repeat from ★ 2 times **more**, skip next sc, (sc in next sc, work Picot, skip next sc) across; join with slip st to first sc, finish off.

Design by Melissa Leapman.

rosebuds

EASY Finished Size: 31¼" x 42¾" (79.5 cm x 108.5 cm)

Shown on page 24.

SHOPPING LIST

Yarn (Medium Weight) 4
[6 ounces, 315 yards
(170.1 grams, 288 meters)
per skein]:
☐ White - 4 skeins
☐ Yellow - 1 skein
☐ Pink - 1 skein
☐ Green - 1 skein
☐ Purple - 1 skein

Crochet Hook
☐ Size G (4 mm)
 or size needed for gauge

GAUGE INFORMATION

In pattern, 12 dc = 3¼" (8.25 cm);
  6 rows = 2½" (6.25 cm)
Gauge Swatch: 3¼" wide x 2½" high
  (8.25 cm x 6.25 cm)
With White, ch 15.
Work same as Body for 6 rows:
5 Clusters and 7 sc.

STITCH GUIDE

CLUSTER (uses one sp)
★ YO, insert hook in sp indicated, YO and pull up a loop, YO and draw through 2 loops on hook; repeat from ★ 3 times **more**, YO and draw through all 5 loops on hook. Push Cluster to **right** side.

COLOR SEQUENCE

4 Rows White, ★ one row Green, one row Pink, 4 rows White, one row Green, one row Yellow, 4 rows White, one row Green, one row Purple, 4 rows White; repeat from ★ throughout, ending by working 4 rows White.

BODY

With White, ch 115, place marker in third ch from hook for st placement.

Row 1 (Right side): 2 Dc in fifth ch from hook (**4 skipped chs count as first dc and one skipped ch**), (skip next ch, 2 dc in next ch) across to last 2 chs, skip next ch, dc in last ch: 112 dc.

Note: Loop a short piece of yarn around any stitch to mark Row 1 as **right** side.

Rows 2-4: Ch 3 (**counts as first dc, now and throughout**), turn; skip next dc, 2 dc in sp **before** next dc *(Fig. 6, page 31)*, ★ skip next 2 dc, 2 dc in sp **before** next dc; repeat from ★ across to last 2 dc, skip next dc, dc in last dc.

Finish off.

Row 5: With **right** side facing, join Green with dc in first dc *(see Joining With Dc, page 30)*; skip next dc, 2 dc in sp **before** next dc, ★ skip next 2 dc, 2 dc in sp **before** next dc; repeat from ★ across to last 2 dc, skip next dc, dc in last dc; finish off.

Row 6: With **wrong** side facing, join next color with sc in first dc *(see Joining With Sc, page 30)*; sc in sp **before** next dc, work Cluster in sp **before** next dc, ★ sc in sp **before** next dc, work Cluster in sp **before** next dc; repeat from ★ across to last 2 dc, skip next dc, sc in last dc; finish off: 55 Clusters and 57 sc.

Row 7: With **right** side facing, join White with dc in first sc; 2 dc in next Cluster, ★ skip next sc, 2 dc in next Cluster; repeat from ★ across to last 2 sc, skip next sc, dc in last sc; do **not** finish off: 112 dc.

Rows 8-10: Ch 3, turn; skip next dc, 2 dc in sp **before** next dc, ★ skip next 2 dc, 2 dc in sp **before** next dc; repeat from ★ across to last 2 dc, skip next dc, dc in last dc.

Finish off.

Continuing to follow color sequence, repeat Rows 5-10 for pattern until Body measures approximately 41¾" (106 cm), ending by working Row 10; do **not** finish off.

EDGING

Rnd 1: Ch 1, turn; 3 sc in first dc, 2 sc in next dc, sc in next dc and in each dc across to last dc, 3 sc in last dc; work 155 sc evenly spaced across ends of rows; working in free loops of beginning ch *(Fig. 3, page 30)*, 3 sc in first ch, 2 sc in next ch, sc in each ch across to marked ch, 3 sc in marked ch; work 155 sc evenly spaced across ends of rows; join with slip st to first sc: 544 sc.

Rnd 2: Ch 1, turn; sc in same st as joining and in each sc around working 3 sc in center sc of each corner 3-sc group; join with slip st to first sc: 552 sc.

Rnd 3: Ch 1, turn; (sc, ch 2, sc) in each of next 3 sc (corner 3-sc group), ★ skip next sc, † (sc, ch 2, sc) in next sc, skip next sc †; repeat from † to † across to next corner 3-sc group, (sc, ch 2, sc) in each of next 3 sc; repeat from ★ 2 times **more**, skip next sc, repeat from † to † across; join with slip st to first sc, finish off.

Design by Melissa Leapman.

square-in-square

EASY   **Finished Size:** 33" x 43" (84 cm x 109 cm)

SHOPPING LIST

Yarn (Medium Weight) 🧶
[3.5 ounces, 246 yards
(100 grams, 225 meters) per skein]:
- ☐ Blue - 6 skeins
- ☐ Dark Blue - 4 skeins

Crochet Hook
- ☐ Size I (5.5 mm)
  or size needed for gauge

GAUGE INFORMATION

In pattern, 12 sts = 3⅛" (8 cm);
  12 rows = 2¾" (7 cm)
Gauge Swatch: 4" wide x 2¾" high
  (10 cm x 7 cm)
With Blue, ch 16.
Work same as Body for 12 rows:
12 sts and 3 ch-1 sps.

Each row is worked across length of the Body. When joining yarn and finishing off, leave a 7" (18 cm) length to be worked into fringe.

BODY

With Blue, ch 166, place marker in second ch from hook for st placement.

Row 1 (Right side)**:** Sc in second ch from hook and in each ch across; finish off: 165 sc.

Note: Loop a short piece of yarn around any stitch to mark Row 1 as **right** side.

Row 2: With **wrong** side facing, join Dark Blue with sc in first sc *(see Joining With Sc, page 30)*; ★ ch 1, skip next st, sc in next sc; repeat from ★ across; finish off: 83 sc and 82 ch-1 sps.

Row 3: With **right** side facing, join Blue with sc in first sc; ★ working **behind** next ch-1, dc in skipped st one row **below**, sc in next sc; repeat from ★ across; finish off: 165 sts.

Row 4: Repeat Row 2: 83 sc and 82 ch-1 sps.

Row 5: With **right** side facing, join Blue with sc in first sc; ★ working in **front** of next ch-1, dc in skipped dc one row **below**, sc in next sc; repeat from ★ across; finish off: 165 sts.

Rows 6 and 7: Repeat Rows 2 and 3: 165 sts.

Row 8: With **wrong** side facing, join Dark Blue with sc in first sc; ch 1, skip next dc, ★ sc in next 5 sts, ch 1, skip next dc; repeat from ★ across to last sc, sc in last sc; finish off: 137 sc and 28 ch-1 sps.

Row 9: With **right** side facing, join Blue with sc in first sc; working in **front** of each ch-1, dc in skipped dc one row **below**, ★ ch 1, skip next sc, sc in next 3 sc, ch 1, skip next sc, dc in skipped dc one row **below**; repeat from ★ across to last sc, sc in last sc; finish off: 111 sts and 54 ch-1 sps.

26   www.leisurearts.com

Row 10: With **wrong** side facing, join Dark Blue with sc in first sc; ★ ch 1, skip next dc, working **behind** next ch-1, dc in skipped sc one row **below**, ch 1, skip next sc, sc in next sc, ch 1, skip next sc, working **behind** next ch-1, dc in skipped sc one row **below**; repeat from ★ across to last 2 sts, ch 1, skip next dc, sc in last sc; finish off: 83 sts and 82 ch-1 sps.

Row 11: With **right** side facing, join Blue with sc in first sc; working in **front** of next ch-1, dc in skipped dc one row **below**, ★ ch 1, skip next dc, working in **front** of next ch-1, dc in skipped sc one row **below**, sc in next sc, working in **front** of next ch-1, dc in skipped sc one row **below**, ch 1, skip next dc, working in **front** of next ch-1, dc in skipped dc one row **below**; repeat from ★ across to last sc, sc in last sc; finish off: 111 sts and 54 ch-1 sps.

Row 12: With **wrong** side facing, join Dark Blue with sc in first sc; ★ ch 1, skip next dc, working **behind** next ch-1, dc in skipped dc one row **below**, sc in next 3 sts, working **behind** next ch-1, dc in skipped dc one row **below**; repeat from ★ across to last 2 sts, ch 1, skip next dc, sc in last sc; finish off: 137 sts and 28 ch-1 sps.

Row 13: With **right** side facing, join Blue with sc in first sc; working in **front** of next ch-1, dc in skipped dc one row **below**, ★ sc in next 5 sts, working in **front** of next ch-1, dc in skipped dc one row **below**; repeat from ★ across to last sc, sc in last sc; finish off: 165 sts.

Rows 14-139: Repeat Rows 2-13, 10 times; then repeat Rows 2-7 once **more**: 165 sts.

TRIM
FIRST SIDE
Row 1: With **wrong** side facing, join Blue with sc in first sc; sc in next dc, ★ ch 1, skip next sc, sc in next dc; repeat from ★ across to last sc, sc in last sc; finish off: 84 sc and 81 ch-1 sps.

Row 2: With **right** side facing, join Blue with slip st in first sc; ch 2, (slip st in next ch-1 sp, ch 2) across to last 2 sc, skip next sc, slip st in last sc; finish off.

SECOND SIDE
Row 1: With **wrong** side facing and working in free loops of beginning ch *(Fig. 3, page 30)*, join Blue with sc in marked ch; sc in next ch, ★ ch 1, skip next ch, sc in next ch; repeat from ★ across to last ch, sc in last ch; finish off: 84 sc and 81 ch-1 sps

Row 2: With **right** side facing, join Blue with slip st in first sc; ch 2, (slip st in next ch-1 sp, ch 2) across to last 2 sc, skip next sc, slip st in last sc; finish off.

FRINGE
Cut a piece of cardboard 7" (18 cm) square.
Wind the desired color of yarn **loosely** and **evenly** around the cardboard until the card is filled, then cut across one end; repeat as needed.
Hold 2 strands of corresponding color yarn together. With **wrong** side facing and using a crochet hook, draw the folded end up through the row and pull all loose ends through the folded end *(Fig. A)*; draw the knot up tightly *(Fig. B)*. Repeat in end of each row along short edges of Body. Lay flat on a hard surface and trim the ends.

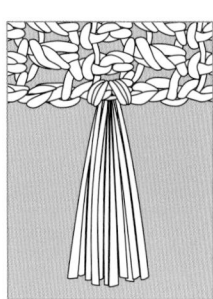

Fig. A   Fig. B

Design by Anne Halliday.

general instructions

ABBREVIATIONS

BPdc	Back Post double crochet(s)
ch(s)	chain(s)
cm	centimeters
dc	double crochet(s)
dc2tog	double crochet 2 together
dc3tog	double crochet 3 together
FPdc	Front Post double crochet(s)
FPdtr	Front Post double treble crochet(s)
hdc	half double crochet(s)
mm	millimeters
Rnd(s)	Round(s)
sc	single crochet(s)
sc2tog	single crochet 2 together
sp(s)	space(s)
st(s)	stitch(es)
tr	treble crochet(s)
YO	yarn over

SYMBOLS & TERMS

★ — work instructions following ★ as many **more** times as indicated in addition to the first time.

† to † or ♥ to ♥ — work all instructions from first † to second † **or** from first ♥ to second ♥ **as many** times as specified.

( ) or [ ] — work enclosed instructions **as many** times as specified by the number immediately following **or** contains explanatory remarks.

colon (:) — the number(s) given after a colon at the end of a row or round denote(s) the number of stitches or spaces you should have on that row or round.

GAUGE

Exact gauge is **essential** for proper size. Before beginning your project, make the sample swatch given in the individual instructions in the yarn and hook specified. After completing the swatch, measure it, counting your stitches and rows carefully. If your swatch is larger or smaller than specified, **make another, changing hook size to get the correct gauge.** Keep trying until you find the size hook that will give you the specified gauge.

Yarn Weight Symbol & Names	LACE 0	SUPER FINE 1	FINE 2	LIGHT 3	MEDIUM 4	BULKY 5	SUPER BULKY 6	JUMBO 7
Type of Yarns in Category	Fingering, size 10 crochet thread	Sock, Fingering, Baby	Sport, Baby	DK, Light Worsted	Worsted, Afghan, Aran	Chunky, Craft, Rug	Super Bulky, Roving	Jumbo, Roving
Crochet Gauge* Ranges in Single Crochet to 4" (10 cm)	32-42 sts**	21-32 sts	16-20 sts	12-17 sts	11-14 sts	8-11 sts	6-9 sts	5 sts and fewer
Advised Hook Size Range	Steel*** 6 to 8, Regular hook B 1	B-1 to E-4	E-4 to 7	7 to I-9	I-9 to K-10½	K-10½ to M/N-13	M/N-13 to Q	Q and larger

*GUIDELINES ONLY: The chart above reflects the most commonly used gauges and hook sizes for specific yarn categories.

** Lace weight yarns are usually crocheted with larger hooks to create lacy openwork patterns. Accordingly, a gauge range is difficult to determine. Always follow the gauge stated in your pattern.

*** Steel crochet hooks are sized differently from regular hooks–the higher the number, the smaller the hook, which is the reverse of regular hook sizing.

CROCHET TERMINOLOGY

UNITED STATES		INTERNATIONAL
slip stitch (slip st)	=	single crochet (sc)
single crochet (sc)	=	double crochet (dc)
half double crochet (hdc)	=	half treble crochet (htr)
double crochet (dc)	=	treble crochet (tr)
treble crochet (tr)	=	double treble crochet (dtr)
double treble crochet (dtr)	=	triple treble crochet (ttr)
triple treble crochet (tr tr)	=	quadruple treble crochet (qtr)
skip	=	miss

CROCHET HOOKS

U.S.	B-1	C-2	D-3	E-4	F-5	G-6	7	H-8	I-9	J-10	K-10½	L-11	M/N-13	N/P-15	P/Q	Q	S
Metric - mm	2.25	2.75	3.25	3.5	3.75	4	4.5	5	5.5	6	6.5	8	9	10	15	16	19

MARKERS

Markers are used to help distinguish the beginning of each round being worked. Place a 2" (5 cm) scrap piece of yarn before the first stitch of each round, moving the marker after each round is complete.

JOINING WITH SC

When instructed to join with sc, begin with a slip knot on hook. Insert hook in stitch or space indicated, YO and pull up a loop, YO and draw through both loops on hook.

JOINING WITH HDC

When instructed to join with dc, begin with a slip knot on hook. YO, holding loop on hook, insert hook in stitch or space indicated, YO and pull up a loop, YO and draw through all 3 loops on hook.

JOINING WITH DC

When instructed to join with dc, begin with a slip knot on hook. YO, holding loop on hook, insert hook in stitch or space indicated, YO and pull up a loop (3 loops on hook), (YO and draw through 2 loops on hook) twice.

BACK RIDGE OF A CHAIN

Work only in loops indicated by arrows *(Fig. 1)*.

Fig. 1

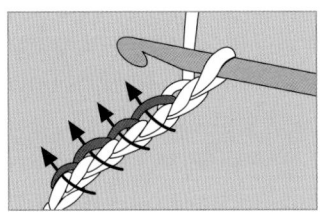

BACK LOOPS ONLY

Work only in loop(s) indicated by arrow *(Fig. 2)*.

Fig. 2

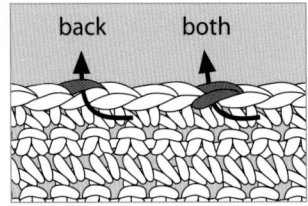

FREE LOOPS OF A CHAIN

When instructed to work in free loops of a chain, work in loop indicated by arrow *(Fig. 3)*.

Fig. 3

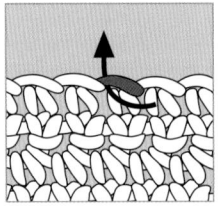

POST STITCH

Work around post of stitch indicated, inserting hook in direction of arrow *(Fig. 4)*.

Fig. 4

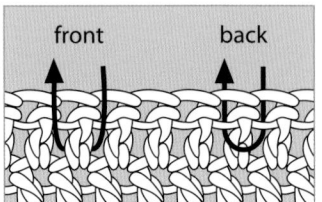

CHANGING COLORS

Work the last stitch to within one step of completion, hook new yarn *(Fig. 5a, or Fig. 5b)* and draw though both loops on hook.

Fig. 5a

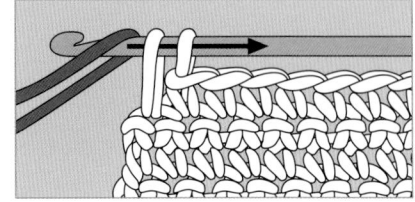

Fig. 5b

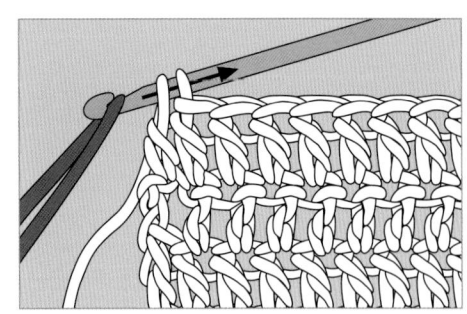

WORKING IN A SPACE BEFORE A STITCH

When instructed to work in a space **before** a stitch or in spaces **between** stitches, insert hook in space indicated by arrow *(Fig. 6)*.

Fig. 6

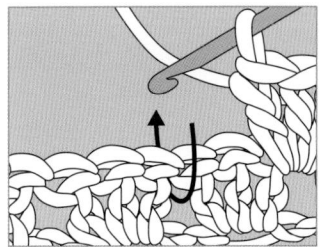

WHIPSTITCH

With **wrong** sides of Blocks, Motifs, Squares, or Strips together, sew through both pieces once to secure the beginning of the seam, leaving an ample yarn end to weave in later. Working through **both** loops of each stitch on **both** pieces *(Fig. 7a)* or through inside loops only of each stitch on **both** pieces *(Fig. 7b)*, insert the needle from **front** to **back** and pull yarn through. ★ Bring the needle around and insert it from **front** to **back** through next stitch and pull yarn through; repeat from ★ across.

Fig. 7a   Fig. 7b

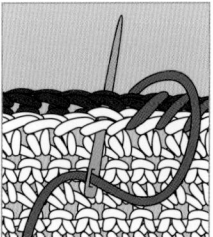

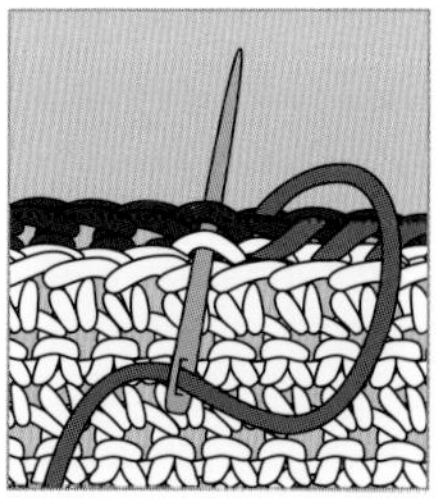

WEAVING SEAMS

With **right** sides of **both** pieces facing you and edges even, sew through both sides once to secure the seam, leaving an ample yarn end to weave in later. Insert the needle from **right** to **left** through one strand on each piece *(Fig. 8)*. Bring the needle around and insert it from **right** to **left** through the next strands on **both** pieces. Continue in this manner, drawing seam together as you work.

Fig. 8

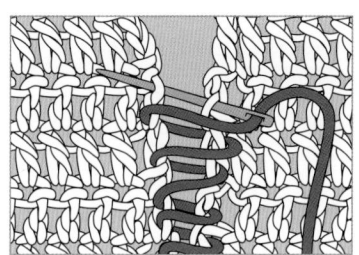

REVERSE HALF DOUBLE CROCHET

(abbreviated reverse hdc)

Working from **left** to **right**, YO, insert hook in st or sp indicated to right of hook *(Fig. 9a)*, YO and draw through, under and to left of loops on hook (3 loops on hook) *(Fig. 9b)*, YO and draw through all 3 loops on hook *(Fig. 9c)* *(reverse hdc made, Fig. 9d)*.

Fig. 9a   Fig. 9b

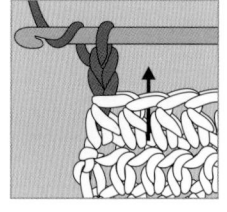 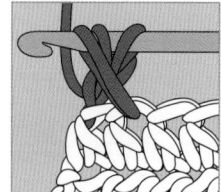

Fig. 9c   Fig. 9d

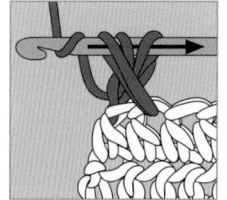 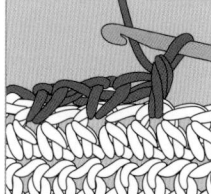

■□□□	BEGINNER	Projects for first-time crocheters using basic stitches. Minimal shaping.
■■□□	EASY	Projects using yarn with basic stitches, repetitive stitch patterns, simple color changes, and simple shaping and finishing.
■■■□	INTERMEDIATE	Projects using a variety of techniques, such as basic lace patterns or color patterns, mid-level shaping and finishing.
■■■■	EXPERIENCED	Projects with intricate stitch patterns, techniques and dimension, such as non-repeating patterns, multi-color techniques, fine threads, small hooks, detailed shaping and refined finishing.

yarn information

The Baby Blankets in this book were made using various weights of yarn. Any brand of the specified yarn weight may be used. It is best to refer to the yardage/meters when determining how many balls or skeins to purchase. Remember, to arrive at the finished size, it is the GAUGE/TENSION that is important, not the brand of yarn.

For your convenience, listed below are the specific yarns used to create our photography models. Because yarn manufacturers make frequent changes in their product lines, you may sometimes find it necessary to use a substitute yarn or to search for the discontinued product at alternate suppliers (locally or online).

ARAN
Bernat® Baby Sport™
#21011 Baby Taupe

DIAMONDS
Red Heart® Baby Hugs™ Light
Grey - #3410 Dolphin
Green - #3562 Aloe
Peach - #3258 Peachie

STRIPES
Lion Brand® Baby Soft®
Peach - #133 Creamsicle
White - #100 White

KALEIDOSCOPE
Bernat® Super Value™
Yellow - #07445 Yellow
Blue - #53725 Hot Blue
Light Blue - #08879 Sky
Dark Blue - #00610 Royal Blue

THERMAL
Bernat® Softee® Baby™
White - #02000 White
Pink - #02001 Pink

HUGS & KISSES
Premier® Cotton Fair®
White - #27-01 White
Blue - #27-04 Turquoise
Yellow - #27-11 Lemon Drops

ROSEBUDS
Caron® Simply Soft®
White - #9701 White
Yellow - #9755 Sunshine
Pink - #0015 Strawberry
Caron® Simply Soft® Brites™
Green - #9607 Limelight
Purple - #9610 Grape

SQUARE-IN-SQUARE
Lion Brand® Jeans®
Blue - #105V Faded
Dark Blue - #110AF Classic

We have made every effort to ensure that these instructions are accurate and complete. We cannot, however, be responsible for human error, typographical mistakes, or variations in individual work.

Blankets made and instructions tested by Janet Akins, Kimberly Holloway, Raymelle Greening, Jerrie Russenberger, Barbara Schou, and Margaret Taverner.

Production Team: Instructional/Technical Writer - Lois J. Long; Senior Graphic Artist - Lora Puls; Graphic Artists - Kytanna McFarlin and Kellie McAnulty; Photo Stylist - Lori Wenger; and Photographer - Jason Masters.

Copyright © 2018 by Leisure Arts, Inc., 104 Champs Blvd., STE 100, Maumelle, AR 72113-6738, www.leisurearts.com. All rights reserved. This publication is protected under federal copyright laws. Reproduction or distribution of this publication or any other Leisure Arts publication, including publications which are out of print, is prohibited unless specifically authorized. This includes, but is not limited to, any form of reproduction or distribution on or through the Internet, including posting, scanning, or e-mail transmission.

Made in U.S.A.